spot

OUTDOOR FUN

CANOEING

by Nessa Black

AMICUS | AMICUS INK

canoe

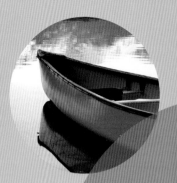

life vest

Look for these words and pictures as you read.

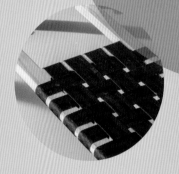

seat

paddle

The lake is still.
It is a good day to canoe.

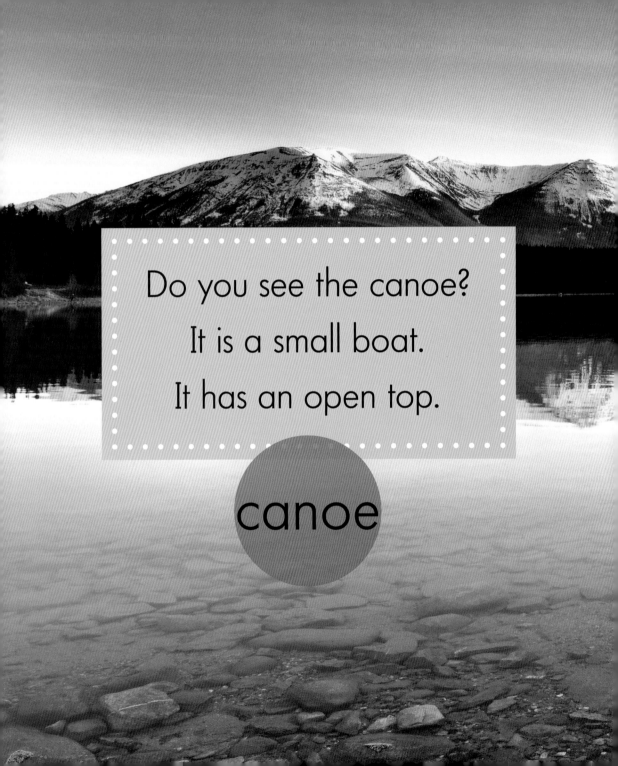

Do you see the canoe?
It is a small boat.
It has an open top.

canoe

Do you see the life vest? Emilia keeps it on. She will float if she falls into the water.

life vest

Max carries the canoe.
This is called portaging.

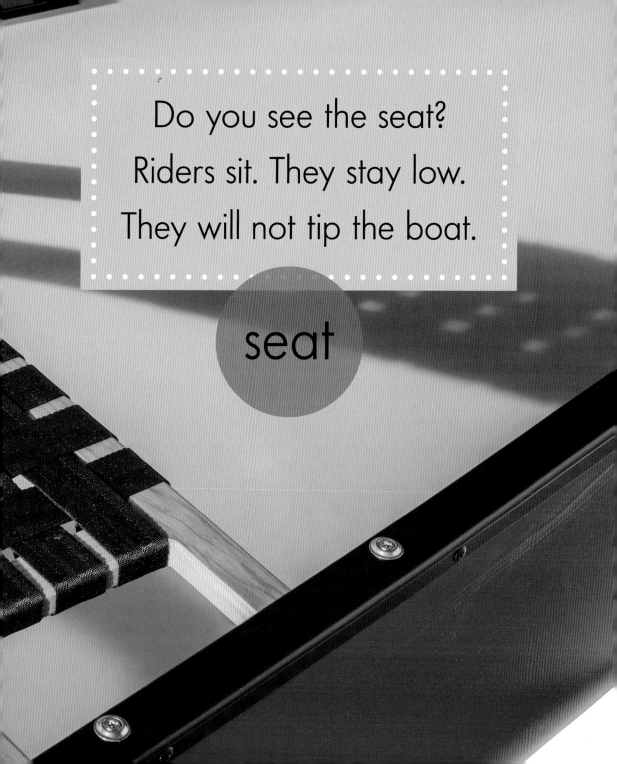

Do you see the seat?
Riders sit. They stay low.
They will not tip the boat.

seat

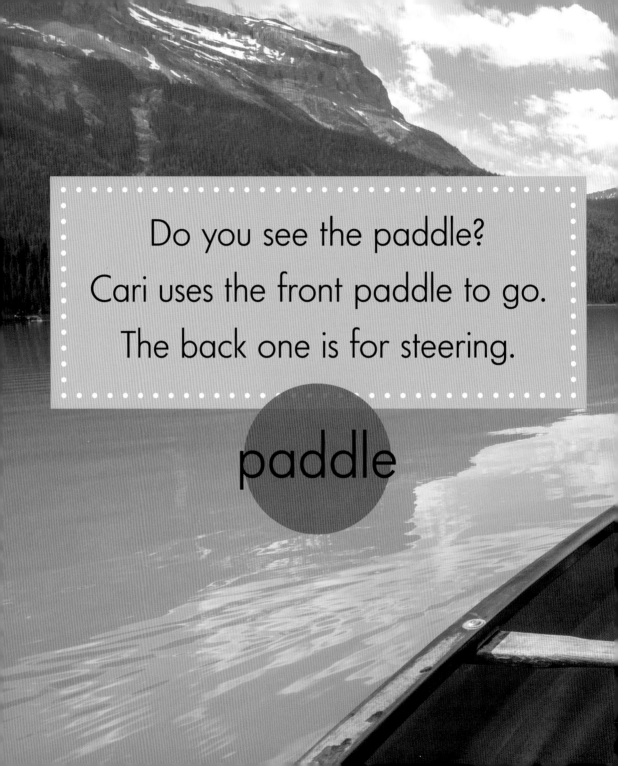

Do you see the paddle?

Cari uses the front paddle to go.

The back one is for steering.

paddle

Eli holds the fishing pole.
The fish are biting. He got one!

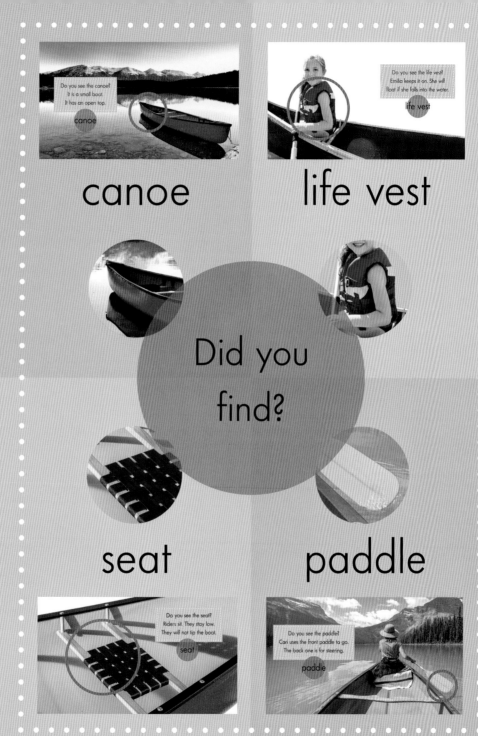

canoe

life vest

Did you find?

seat

paddle

Spot is published by Amicus and Amicus Ink
P.O. Box 1329, Mankato, MN 56002
www.amicuspublishing.us

Library of Congress Cataloging-in-Publication Data
Names: Black, Nessa, author.
Title: Canoeing / by Nessa Black.
Description: Mankato, Minnesota : Amicus, [2020] |
Series: Spot outdoor fun | Audience: Grades:
K to Grade 3.
Identifiers: LCCN 2019003794 (print) | LCCN
2019010810 (ebook) | ISBN 9781681518497 (pdf) |
ISBN 9781681518091(library binding) | ISBN
9781681525372(paperback) | ISBN
9781681518497(eBook)
Subjects: LCSH: Canoes and canoeing--Juvenile literature. |
Vocabulary--Juvenile literature.
Classification: LCC GV784.3 (ebook) | LCC GV784.3 .B53
2020 (print) | DDC 797.122--dc23
LC record available at https://lccn.loc.gov/2019003794

Printed in China

HC 10 9 8 7 6 5 4 3 2 1
PB 10 9 8 7 6 5 4 3 2 1

Wendy Dieker, editor
Deb Miner, series designer
Aubrey Harper, book designer
Shane Freed, photo researcher

Photos by marekuliasz/Shutterstock
cover; DNY59/iStock 1, 16; Hero
Images Inc./Alamy 3; ZCLiu/iStock 4-5;
Lopolo/Dreamstime 6-7; Gary Cook/
Alamy 8-9; Marek Uliasz/Alamy 10-11;
swissmediavision/iStock 12-13; Hero
Images Inc./Alamy 14-15

CANOEING